People and Ur

People have been living in cit
but rural society was the norm. Soon, five billion will live
in urban areas. A massive social change is taking place.

The urbanisation of the world

Every country in the world shows increasing urbanisation, though rates differ from place to place. Africa has seen particularly rapid growth in its cities. For example, the population of Lagos grew from 288,000 in 1950 to over 10 million by 1995 (with 21 million forecast by 2010).

Rapidly growing urbanisation has increased the importance of city health issues. World Health Day (7 April 1996) provided a focus for the WHO's Healthy Cities Programme, whose model for promoting urban health has been adopted by over 1,000 cities worldwide.

A global network is emerging, dealing with urban management 'best practice'. Led by the UN through its various agencies – the WHO, the UN Centre for Human Settlements (UNCHS), the UN Development Programme, the International Labour Organisation and the World Bank – the network includes numerous government and local municipal authorities, non-governmental organisations and private firms.

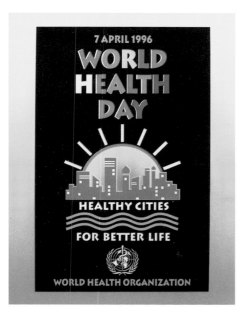

In 1900 only about 14% of the world's people lived in cities. By 1950 the proportion had grown to 29% and by 1995 to 45%. By 2025, the UN estimates that over 61% of all the world's people (forecast at 8.5 billion by then) will be living in urban areas. In other words, 5 billion people will be living in cities (compared with about 2.6 billion in 1995).

The rural predominance of human society, which had persisted from the earliest times until the last few decades, has been transformed. A consequence of the Industrial Revolution, which at first affected only a minority of the world's people, urbanisation is arguably the biggest social change since the development of agriculture.

The reasons for the accelerating pace of urbanisation are many and complex. (They were discussed in *UGI* under the title *World Urbanisation: The dominance of the city*, published in 1992). Whatever the causes, urbanisation appears irreversible. Even the draconian measures taken by China to repopulate the countryside after the Cultural Revolution of the late 1960s provided only a temporary interruption in the general trend towards urbanisation. Mao's nation of peasants is rapidly turning into a population of town dwellers.

In a recent article in *Habitat Debate*, the magazine of the UNCHS, Daniel Biau, head of the agency's Technical Co-operation Division, argued that urbanisation helps to promote economic and social development. Instead of trying to reverse the flow of people from rural areas to cities, international efforts should be focused on making cities work better.

Both GNP per capita and the UN's 'human development index' for a country have almost always improved as urbanisation has proceeded. Cities stimulate the rural economy, lessen pressure on fragile ecological zones and lead to reduced rates of population growth (by providing better living standards and greater educational opportunities for women).

After several decades of grappling with urbanisation in the developing world, there is now a broad measure of agreement on what it takes to manage cities successfully. Six crucial elements can be identified:

decentralisation – local municipal authorities should be given the power to govern cities, with full support from central government;
community participation – local democracy and collective participation are essential to good city management;
economic opportunity – strong efforts should be made to stimulate the local economy so as to create jobs in both formal and informal sectors, and thus reduce poverty;
infrastructure – public/private partnerships should be used to put in place efficient systems for roads, water, energy supply, public transport and waste management;
land rights – should encourage private investment, while protecting the environment, security and public health;
municipal finances – should be transparent, with local property and land taxes fair and coherent.

Cities as diverse as Curitiba (Brazil), Puerta Princesa (Philippines) and Cox's Bazaar (Bangladesh) show that the application of such theories makes good practical sense.

City Food and Water

A city which grows too fast may find it difficult to supply its inhabitants with the most basic necessities for survival – nutritious food and clean water.

Clean water – the most important medical aid

Water-borne diseases account for over half the illnesses and deaths which afflict mankind. Merely providing a clean water supply can have a dramatic impact on community health in the developing world.

Clean water and sanitation are the two most important factors in urban health. Taken for granted in the developed world, they remain a high but unfulfilled priority for poorer countries. Worldwide, over 700 million urban dwellers have no access to clean water and 900 million have no proper sanitation. Figures for the rural community are far worse. (*UGI* dealt with this issue in 1992 under the title *Water and Health*.)

The provision of clean water has long been a primary goal of the United Nations, and the World Health Organisation in particular. In a major effort to improve the lot of the poor in the developing world, some 1,200 million people were provided with clean water during the 1980s – designated by the UN as the International Drinking Water Supply and Sanitation Decade (IDWSSD). Some 770 million people were provided with sanitation (i.e., an acceptable form of excreta disposal). Because of increases in population, however, the number of people without adequate sanitation remained about the same (about 2.3 billion) in 1990 as in 1980.

Those in urban areas were much more likely than their rural cousins to have access to clean water and sanitation. By 1990 some 85% of the developing world's urban population had access to clean water and 74% to sanitation. Percentages in the rural areas were much lower – 59% for water supply, 40% for sanitation. The WHO rightly regards clean water and sanitation as essential starting points for health, yet the targets for 100% coverage by 2000 remain daunting – and almost certainly unachievable, given the other pressures on international aid. Water will need to be supplied to another 775 million people in cities and 1,400 million in rural areas, while sanitation will have to be brought to 915 million urbanites and 1,915 million rural dwellers.

The cost of providing these basic services is immense – some $134 billion was spent in the 1980s, a third of it provided by international aid. But cities have the advantage that urban investment reaches a higher concentration of people. More citizens can be helped for a given sum of money than in the more widely dispersed habitations of the countryside.

WHO photo by L. Taylor

Tokyo, centre of the world's biggest metropolitan area

The urban agglomeration between Tokyo and Yokohama accommodates some 27 million people, making it the biggest metropolitan area in the world. Despite overcrowding and high prices, Tokyo manages to provide most of its citizens with a reasonable quality of life. Unemployment is low (less than 5%), wealth distribution well-balanced and medical care first-class. Its infant mortality record is excellent (5 per 1,000 live births compared with about 100 in Karachi) and its crime rate is extremely low (for example less than 2 murders a year per 100,000 people, compared with over 30 in Rio de Janeiro).

The Tokyo-Kawasaki-Yokohama region includes the Keihin Industrial Zone, the manufacturing heartland of Japan. In the 1970s, urban air pollution was so bad that the city installed coin-in-the-slot oxygen machines on the sidewalks. Unleaded petrol, introduced in 1975, helped to alleviate the problem, as did the move from coal to low-sulphur power stations and stringent new controls over industrial emissions.

As in California, earthquake is an ever-present threat. The Great Earthquake of 1923 destroyed much of the city and killed or injured 100,000 people. A major quake today could be catastrophic, despite improvements in building strength.

Tokyo has no single 'downtown area' but is dotted with urban centres, usually based on railway stations. The city has a dense network of rail lines, underground metros, bus lines and highways. There are numerous small parks.

Healthy food – nutrition and energy

In Western cities, especially in the US, obesity is common. On the other hand, in some cities in Africa, Asia and Latin America, half the population is malnourished. What is the best way to distribute food to a large and fast-growing urban population – via the free market or with government hand-outs? Will 'junk food' replace fresh market produce in the diets of Third World citizens? What will be the effect on their health?

An important indicator of a city's general health is the cost of food. If an average citizen has to spend half of his or her income simply to buy food, provision for other items – housing, clothing, medical services, transport, leisure – is bound to be inadequate. In affluent cities such as Sydney, New York or London, food takes up about 15% of the average household budget. In poor cities like Lagos or Dhaka over 60% of household income goes on food.

Getting beyond the subsistence level is a dream which many millions never fulfil. Can urbanisation, combined with effective city management, break this cycle of despair? Can the experience of Singapore, which transformed itself in a few decades from poverty-stricken slums to sleek high-tech city, be reproduced in other situations? Some believe it could. Although Singapore's combination of strategic location, strong leadership, lack of corruption, communal work ethic and manageable size is not universally shared – and its authoritarian style is not universally admired – the emphasis on planning, education, infrastructure and free market forces has had wide influence.

In the 'post-communist' world, the free market system has gained wide acceptance. At its simplest level, food produced outside a city is

brought into street markets where it is sold to urban inhabitants. Controls over such markets seek to ensure that the food on display is clean and edible. The WHO runs a healthy marketplace programme addressing the health conditions of stall-holders and food handlers. Government inspectors are urged to advise rather than punish, helping market workers to understand the importance of basic hygiene procedures in the handling of foodstuffs, and the safe disposal of food and packaging waste.

One example of what can be done to improve food supply to the urban poor is provided by the Programa Alimentario Integral y Solidario (the PAIS Plan) in Buenos Aires. Launched in 1989, the plan brought together regional government, local NGOs and community residents to help the city's poor. The PAIS Plan is organised into three stages – the setting up of community kitchens (each of which has a financing arrangement with a private bank); the provision of flour, seeds and home machinery to encourage self-production; and the organisation of small businesses (vegetable gardens on vacant lots, food processing and distribution, etc.). This is one of the many innovations which is being studied by experts to see how it might be applied in other countries.

Environmentalists have long encouraged the idea of city allotments and gardens being used to grow food. In some parts of Africa this notion has taken the form of mini-farms within urban areas, a sort of greening of the city, as rural migrants apply their agricultural skills within metropolitan boundaries. Such a development is preferable to the dense accumulation of shacks which characterise all too many cities in the developing world.

All cities benefit from their green spaces. Grass and trees are pleasing on the eye and help to clean urban air. Sometimes, however, food production has an even higher priority.

Market stalls are an important food source in many cities and often provide a direct link with the rural economy. Protection of health requires careful monitoring of hygiene standards in all food-handling activities, especially in warmer climates.

Waste Management

Cities produce vast amounts of human and other waste. How can it best be dealt with? And how can urban air pollution be minimised?

What happens to solid and liquid waste?

Adequate systems for dealing with human excrement and household waste are a basic requirement of good city management. Without them, no city can expect to be healthy.

In the developed world, citizens expect their taxes to cover the cost of waste removal and disposal. For most householders, the accumulation of garbage never goes beyond a week or two. It is then whisked away to unseen disposal sites. For most citizens, municipal waste is largely "out of sight, out of mind".

In poorer countries, waste is all too visible. It is often left to pile up in the streets, simply because no-one can afford to pay for its removal. Scavengers take away all useful material, but leave the rest to rot. With the increasing use of plastics and other non-degradable materials, city waste which was once consumed by nature now just accumulates. Attempts to burn it where it lies may result in clouds of poisonous smoke.

Public waste disposal in developing countries is rarely efficient. Lack of proper maintenance often means that 20-50% of garbage trucks are out of service. When the city of Dar es Salaam in Tanzania bought 30

garbage trucks in 1987 it seemed as if a big improvement was underway. By 1992, however, only three were still in service, the rest having been cannibalised for spare parts.

Similar stories come from many other cities. High-profile capital spending can win votes or prestige for local politicians and may be attractive to international donors wishing to make a visible impact. Putting in place the factors needed to ensure efficient long-term operation is an altogether different and more complex task. This requires not just money but organising skill, a corruption-free environment and commitment from those directly involved. Hence the move towards privatisation of waste collection and other municipal services, where the profit motive provides an incentive.

The danger of corruption (bribes account for 10-30% of waste contract costs in some countries) may be reduced by competitive tendering and transparent, accountable

Efficient collection and disposal of waste are essential for a healthy urban environment. In many cities in the developing world, 20-50% of all rubbish generated is left to accumulate in the streets, attracting vermin and disease.

Richard Buckley

The Zabbaleen in Cairo

For centuries the Zabbaleen 'scavengers' have scraped a living by collecting and sorting rubbish collected from the streets of Cairo. In recent years, this activity has been given positive encouragement by the authorities, thus transforming what was a subsistence activity tolerated by the city into a profitable and mutually beneficial venture. Cairo's waste disposal services have been improved, while the status and living standards of the Zabbaleen, largely members of a Coptic Christian underclass, have been enhanced.

The Cairo city authorities have allocated areas of unused land to the Zabbaleen to use as storage and sorting areas. Organic waste is fed to the Zabbaleen's pigs, thus providing a valuable food source for the non-Muslim population. Other waste is carefully sorted and recycled into products which can be traded or sold in Cairo. Examples include shoes, textiles and tinware. Some 50 recycling/manufacturing businesses have been launched, with non-profit organisations sometimes providing basic skills, equipment and start-up funds. The Mega-Cities Project*, with funding from the UN, has worked to set up similar programmes in Manila and Bombay.

Is the air fit to breathe?

In many cities air quality falls well below international health standards. All over the world, people – and especially children – are being slowly poisoned by the very air they breathe. Pollutants include lead, carbon monoxide, photochemical smog, sulphur dioxide, volatile organic compounds, and small particulates. Air pollution is hard to measure and control, and is still not taken seriously enough by many governments.

Like many of the world's biggest cities, Cairo suffers from heavy air pollution caused by vehicle emissions and local industry (e.g., cement and steel). The air over Cairo has a high concentration of particulate matter, much of it blown in from the surrounding desert. Cairo also has a large population of old taxis, buses and trucks. Two-thirds of Cairo's million vehicles are more than ten years old. New emission standards are expected to improve matters, as will the change from coal to gas at local power stations.

As in other cities, the growth in vehicle numbers threatens to outpace govern-ment measures to improve air quality. Some cities are introducing more radical solutions, including road pricing, bans on private cars, low or zero emission requirements ('electric cars') and better public transport systems.

systems. Using different private contractors in different zones, perhaps in competition with public authority collectors, is another safeguard against corruption and inefficiency. Cities as different as Bogotá and Phoenix use this kind of approach. To help smaller companies get in on the act, some Dutch cities add to the final contract the tendering costs of other bidders. In this way smaller companies can afford to compete with the largest.

Hazardous waste is becoming an increasing problem in countries which are adopting Western-style consumerism. Municipal waste may contain a wide variety of toxic materials – batteries, insecticides, cleaning fluids, adhesives and so on. Ideally, toxic waste should be separated from non-hazardous organic waste but this doesn't always happen even in rich countries. In poor countries, mixed waste is routinely piled in heaps, often close to waterways and human settlements. Contamination of groundwater is a serious problem.

While high-temperature incineration is increasingly used in developed countries as a way to get rid of non-recyclable waste, such high-tech solutions may not be appropriate or affordable in the developing world.

Nor can the poorer countries afford the emission reduction technologies which have helped to clean up the air in many western cities. The air in a large Chinese city has 14 times the amount of suspended particulates as that in an American city. Like London in the early part of the 20th century, Chinese cities typically depend on coal for energy production. Emissions of sulphur dioxide and soot are therefore high. As energy demand soars, air pollution can be expected to deteriorate further.

But this is not inevitable. London stopped its killer smogs by banning coal fires. Los Angeles wants to bring in zero emission cars as a way to combat pollution. The technological knowledge is available, but what about political will?

Big cities have much to learn from each other. Indeed, it has been argued that the world's mega-cities have more in common with each other than with small towns in their own countries. The networking and exchange of ideas between urban managers in different parts of the world is gathering momentum, aided by the UN and by organisations such as the Mega-Cities Project*, the International Union of Local Author-ities and the International Society of City and Regional Planners.

Mexico City – living with the world's most polluted urban air

As far as air quality is concerned, Mexico City is perhaps the least healthy city in the world. It sits in a bowl among high mountains, a natural reservoir for the collection of bad air. Because of its altitude (2,250 metres above sea level), the oxygen content of Mexico City's air is lower than in most other large cities. Motor vehicles (the city has 3 million of them) are forced to use richer fuel mixtures than normal, adding to the problem of exhaust emissions. Leaded petrol is still widely used. Industrial pollution, fecal dust and butene from domestic stoves add to the toxic content of the city's air. Breathing it is said to be equivalent to inhaling 40 cigarettes a day. Vegetables and fruit grown on the outskirts of the city are often contaminated with heavy metals and other poisons. Other problems include the large amounts of illegally dumped or uncollected waste and the shortage of water, which has to be pumped up to the city from remote valleys, at huge cost.

The city authorities are doing their best to improve the situation, but lack of money is a major constraint. All private vehicles have to be kept off the road for one day a week under the *Hoy No Circula* scheme, with different colour licence plates used to monitor the system. Some industrial plants are temporarily closed down when pollution gets too bad. Since 1991, new cars have had to have catalytic converters. Public transport and goods vehicles are being converted to compressed natural gas or other less polluting fuels.

Serving the People

Cities should be run for the benefit of all those who live in them. Community participation is an essential aspect of a healthy city – but may be hard to achieve.

Access to electric power, telephones and TV

Some 'home comforts' – heat, electricity, television, access to a telephone – are important to urban well-being even in the poorest districts of Third World cities. But other factors – dirt, violence, overcrowding, noise, family and community relationships – may have even greater impact on human health.

The health of urban citizens depends only partly on freedom from disease. Other factors such as social life and employment prospects have an important bearing on an individual's sense of well-being.

Animal pets provide comfort to many city people, but add to the problems of waste disposal and public health. The vast amounts spent on petfood in rich countries contrast with human malnutrition in much of the developing world.

Participation has become the great watchword of international advisers on development projects. "Get the local people involved", they say, "and much more can be achieved." This is encouraging for those who believe in democracy, but the reality is that strong leadership is still needed if participation is to result in effective action, rather than sectional bickering.

Conflict and suspicion between interest groups – central government, city authorities, entrepreneurs, local communities – often has to be overcome before a project can get off the ground. It can take months or even years to build up the mutual trust and respect that is needed. As a recent World Bank publication observed, government may be perceived as corrupt or bureaucratic, business as greedy and uncaring, local communities as too parochial, academic experts as too remote in their 'ivory towers'.

Bringing such groups together requires a big effort and good leadership. Some of the most effective urban programmes have been carried out under strong, energetic mayors. Others have been led by outside 'facilitators' such as NGOs or UN experts.

The transformation of a city is easier if there is some new political situation brought on by elections or a new administration, acting with strong public support. There has to be a tried and tested solution to put in place and some mechanism for linking the problem-solvers with the decision-makers, so that ideas move from debating table to reality.

Whoever provides the leadership, grassroots involvement is vital. Experts and mayors eventually move on. Unless the local people are committed to a project, it will not work. Attempts to bring in services such as water or electricity may founder because the community refuses to pay municipal taxes to help cover the cost – either because they suspect corruption or fail to understand the link between taxation and public services. Building trust between government and the governed is thus a prerequisite of successful urban management.

Electricity is a key service for urban dwellers. Without it, it is hard to live a civilised life. When governments fail to provide electricity in urban slums, local communities often tap into lines illegally, despite the risks. Solar panels may soon make community-generated electricity a feasible option (see *UGI 96/3 Solar Energy*) – and also remove the tangle of dangerous wires which deface

Richard Buckley

Transport systems

Motor vehicles clog the streets of most cities and cause huge loss of productivity and health damage. Bangkok is reckoned to lose a third of city GDP from traffic delays. Congestion costs São Paulo $5 billion a year. In Mexico City, thousands of people are killed by exhaust fumes every year. Leaded fuel, still widely used in the developing world, causes many city children to suffer illness and brain damage. Public transport is therefore a key element in urban health.

urban slums – but demand for electricity is too great to be met by solar power alone. Fossil fuel power stations in the developing world will continue to pollute the air of many cities for years to come.

Public transportation is another key issue in all urban areas. Government planners tend to favour big projects which benefit business or the richer members of the community. In the developing world, undue emphasis is often put on roads and vehicles – even though most of the population cannot afford cars. In Jakarta, a change in transport policy put 60,000 rickshaw operators out of work, removing a non-polluting and labour intensive form of transport from the scene – and abolishing a famous tradition.

In India, oxcarts, donkey carts and human-drawn vehicles are ignored in drawing up transport plans for the future, even though such traditional modes of transport

remain in widespread use – and cause relatively few environmental problems by comparison with motor vehicles. It is not easy for politicians bent on modernisation to espouse 'low-tech' ways of doing things.

Public-private partnerships can be highly effective in transport systems. In some German cities, for example, tickets for public transport can also be used for taxis in off-peak hours. In Singapore, the same tickets are used for subway trains and for private buses. Income is divided between the operators, based on computer records generated when the passenger inserts the ticket into an electronic recorder at each point of use.

'Healthy cities' develop public transport systems using light rail, underground metros and buses, thereby replacing cars as the normal mode of urban transport. Other cities have opted for the motor car – and are now regretting the choice.

Throughput on Curitiba's buses has been increased with the help of 'boarder tubes' which enable passengers to pay the fare before getting on the bus. These boarding tubes have greatly increased the carrying capacity of the bus system. A bus using Curitiba's 'direct route/ boarding tube' system is reckoned to carry three times as many people as a conventional bus on an average street. In 1993 the Mega-Cities Project shipped four of these tubes to New York to demonstrate a rapid metrobus system.

The Curitiba experience – solving the public transport problem

Curitiba in south-eastern Brazil has earned an international reputation for good city management with its innovative programmes for public transport, waste recycling and 'green space'. One of Brazil's fastest-growing cities (population about 2.5 million in 1995), it has avoided many of the problems that usually go with rapid expansion and the breakdown of city services. Early in its development, Curitiba adopted a plan for linear growth along radial axes, using the areas in between for green space and leisure facilities as well as for industrial and housing development.

Curitiba has few traffic jams, despite having more cars per capita than any other Brazilian city except Brasilia. Roads running along the structural axes include special 'busways' which provide rapid transport of people to and from the city centre. Concentric roads link the radial axes with outlying districts. A sophisticated bus system has been developed, featuring red express buses, green inter-district buses and yellow 'feeder' buses. There are regular services, which are closely linked so that it is easy and quick to switch from one route to another. Terminals at 2 km intervals are equipped with newspaper stands, public telephones, post offices and shops. There is a single fare for all journeys within the city limits, with tickets interchangeable on all routes.

The transport network is managed by a city authority which lays down operating rules, sets timetables and routes, and monitors performance. The buses themselves are run by private companies, licensed by the city authority. Each company is paid on the basis of distance travelled. It is a simple, transparent system. And it works. Some 75% of commuters in Curitiba travel by bus. (In Sydney, by contrast, over 60% go to work by car; in Los Angeles 90%.)

Curitiba opted for a bus system, in preference to underground metro or light rail, because it is far cheaper in terms of capital cost. Curitiba is not a rich city. Average income is roughly comparable with that of people living in São Paulo.

Understanding
Global Issues

Figure 1: Urbanisation by country

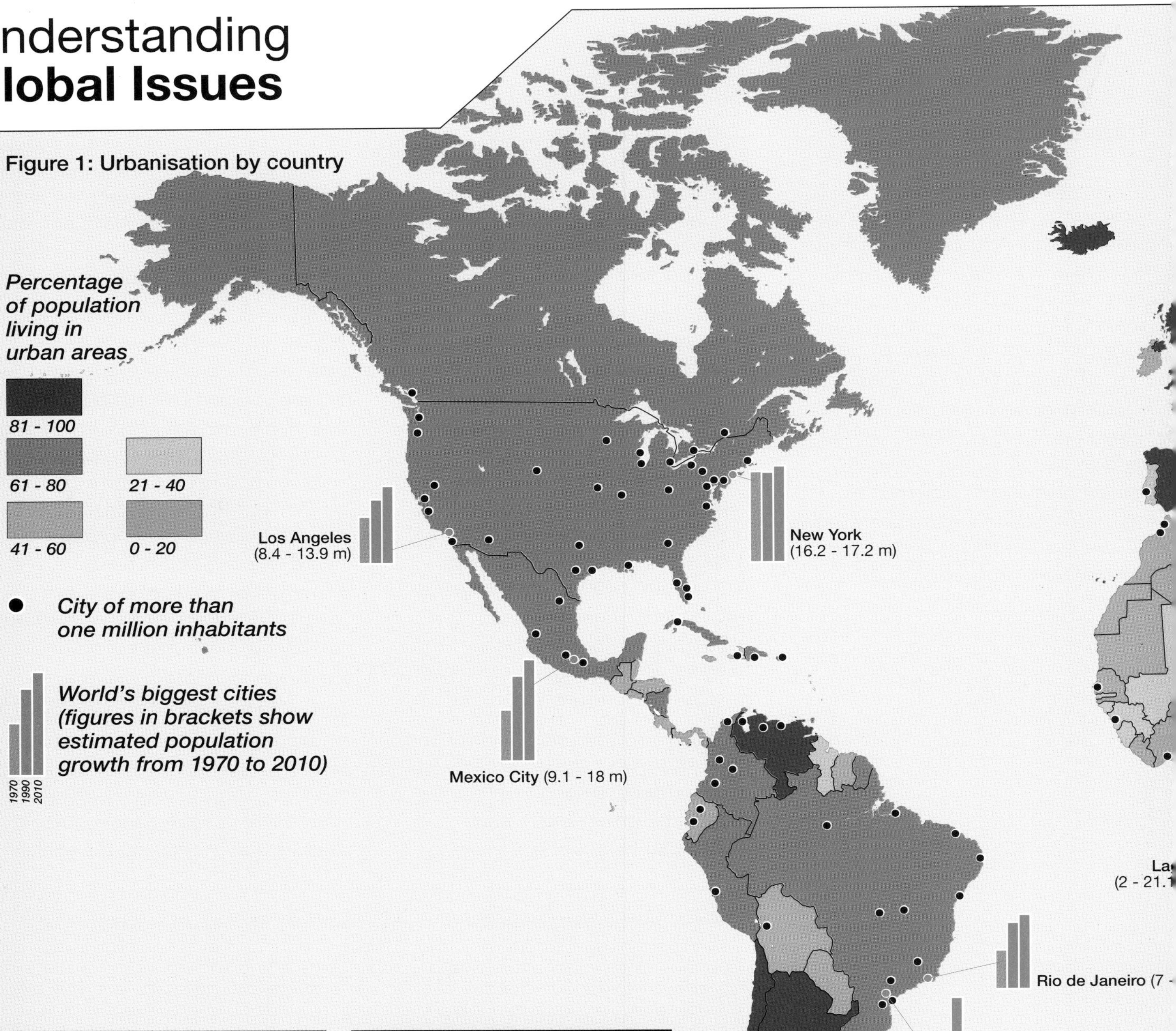

Percentage of population living in urban areas

- 81 - 100
- 61 - 80
- 41 - 60
- 21 - 40
- 0 - 20

● City of more than one million inhabitants

World's biggest cities (figures in brackets show estimated population growth from 1970 to 2010)

1970 1990 2010

Los Angeles (8.4 - 13.9 m)

New York (16.2 - 17.2 m)

Mexico City (9.1 - 18 m)

La[g] (2 - 21.[

Rio de Janeiro (7 -

São Paulo (8.1 - 25 m)

Buenos Aires (8.4 - 13.7 m)

Average living space (persons per room,

Percentage of households with running water

Percentage o[f] household income remaining after paying for food

Air quality

Sources: United Nations and Population Action International (formerly Population Crisis Committttee)

Urbanisation and Health
Wide variations in the quality of city life

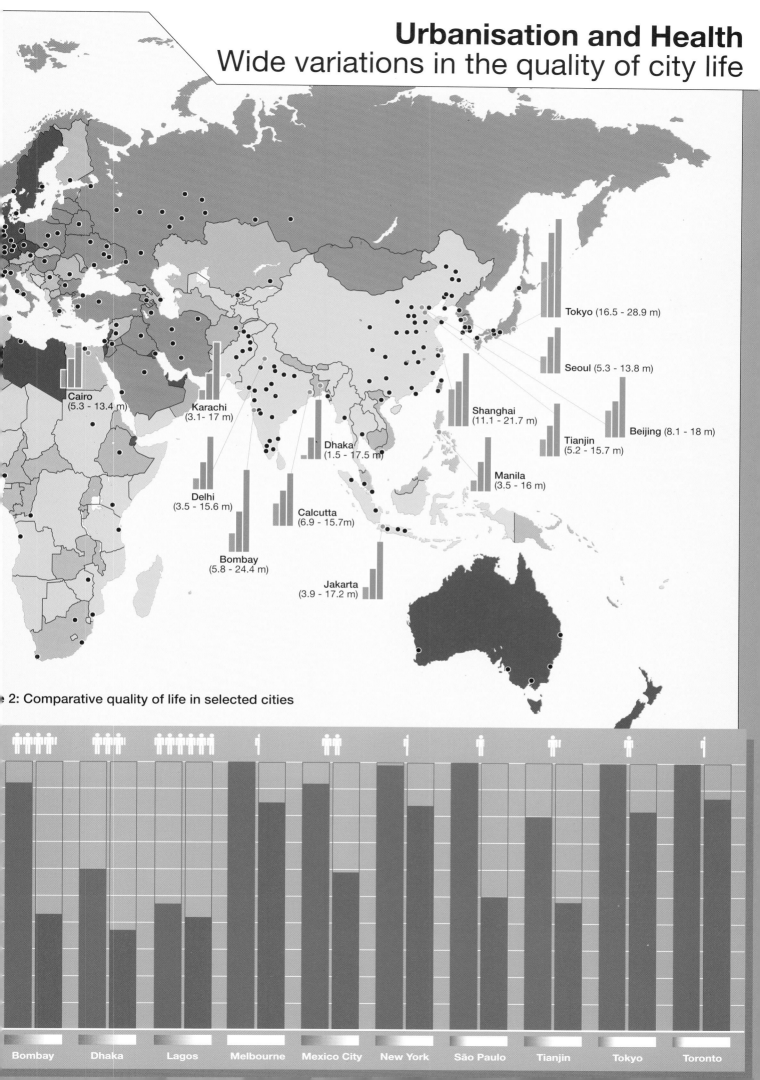

Tokyo (16.5 - 28.9 m)

Seoul (5.3 - 13.8 m)

Beijing (8.1 - 18 m)

Tianjin (5.2 - 15.7 m)

Shanghai (11.1 - 21.7 m)

Cairo (5.3 - 13.4 m)

Karachi (3.1 - 17 m)

Dhaka (1.5 - 17.5 m)

Manila (3.5 - 16 m)

Delhi (3.5 - 15.6 m)

Calcutta (6.9 - 15.7 m)

Bombay (5.8 - 24.4 m)

Jakarta (3.9 - 17.2 m)

2: Comparative quality of life in selected cities

Bombay | Dhaka | Lagos | Melbourne | Mexico City | New York | São Paulo | Tianjin | Tokyo | Toronto

Education for Health

A healthy city is one whose inhabitants have the knowledge and the means to minimise the risks of disease – and respect each other's right to live in peace.

Prevention is better than cure

Many of the world's urban poor are unaware of even the most basic steps for protecting their own health. Hence the emphasis on primary health care programmes. Building hospitals looks good on political manifestos but is not as cost-effective as the harder, long-term slog of educating the public in good health practices – boiling water, washing food and hands, avoiding drugs, practising 'safe sex, eating nutritious food.

In the 1980s in Cali, Colombia, the biggest cause of death among city dwellers was not cancer, respiratory disease or heart failure but murder. As in many other cities, inter-personal violence is a major health hazard. Provision of medical care alleviates the symptoms of this problem but does nothing to deal with the root causes. Building more hospitals to treat citizens wounded by gunshot or knife wounds is not the answer, though more medical facilities are certainly needed.

In this case, the city authorities took some important practical steps to cut down the violence. For example, they imposed a ban on carrying handguns and bladed weapons, placed restrictions on selling alcohol in public places and initiated mass campaigns to promote mutual tolerance. Communal health may have as much to do with social tensions as with medical care.

In many cities, drugs and alcohol account for a high proportion of violent crime. The *machismo* culture which gives men a 'right' to physically abuse their women is another common problem. And changing a culture – whether based on drug-taking, hard drinking or male dominance – is far harder than building a hospital.

Domestic violence is depressingly common throughout the world, with women and children bearing the main brunt of this kind of oppression. No wonder that women are increasingly involved in grassroots movements, aimed at improving both their own rights and health and living conditions generally.

Education is of vital importance in disease prevention, whether the ailment is measles (which kills a million children each year and often causes complications in the other

The education of women is a particularly important aspect of improving urban health in the developing world. Women trained in 'primary health care' play a vital role in the health of their families and communities. Education of women also has a direct impact on population growth, with birth rates dropping as knowledge of contraception and reproductive health increases. However, family units often break down under the pressures of urban living.

In deprived urban areas, vandalism and littering are common – and often carried out by local youngsters who pay scant attention to health care or community values. Yet group loyalty is strong and energy plentiful. How can these qualities be turned to constructive use? Urban health and well-being cannot be divorced from wider social issues, such as youth training and unemployment.

WHO / Ghana Registered Nurses Association

The stresses of urban life – crime, noise, pollution

In some urban environments physical violence is a much greater health hazard than disease. The stresses of urban living – including lack of privacy, proper employment or peace and quiet – turns some to alcohol and drugs. At greatest risk are those – often the poor or disadvantaged – who do not realise the health risks associated with their behaviour.

43 million who catch it), tuberculosis (which afflicts over a billion people worldwide), schistosomiasis, diarrhoea, Aids or any of the other diseases which afflict urban populations. Large-scale immunisation programmes, such as the WHO's recent measles campaign, tend to be more effective in urban areas than in scattered rural communities. Defeating Aids is a far more challenging task, since it involves so many cultural factors.

Children provide the long-term answer to culture change. If they can be taught good health habits, the importance of community responsibility, and the importance of broader environmental considerations, there is hope for the future. The Healthy Cities Foundation of Pécs, Hungary, found that "Pollution and the environment" was ranked by the city's children as the most severe current problem in Hungary, and 66% of them predicted that their health in 25 years will be "greatly affected" by the state of the environment. Such awareness is widespread throughout eastern Europe, though probably not in much of Africa and Latin America, where more immediate concerns, such as getting enough food, often take precedence.

In many cities in the developing world, a large proportion of the

population does not have access to even minimum living standards. They breathe polluted air and drink polluted water. City authorities are unable to cope with demand for clean water, sanitation, electricity, transport, jobs and schools. Children brought up in these conditions have first-hand experience of what environmental degradation means.

In Tehran a healthy cities project included training school children in primary health care. They are encouraged to look after the school and their neighbourhood, by helping to keep the streets clean and setting an example of good hygiene at home. A magazine called *Healthy Message* is used to propagate innovative ideas. There is no political slant to this, just a desire to improve living conditions for the Iranian people.

Despite cultural differences between Iran and the West, the idea of 'healthy cities' has been embraced in Iran with enthusiasm and skill. The conflicts which so often bedevil international politics are largely absent from the forums which bring together the world's urban managers, engineers, scientists and health workers. The personal and institutional networks which are being built up provide an encouraging backdrop to what can sometimes appear to be a dismally divided world.

The use of traditional curatives persists in many cultures. How should such customs be regarded, bearing in mind the demand for 'modern medicine' in the developing world and the West's rediscovery of herbal remedies? Is too much emphasis placed on modern drugs and surgical techniques? Is the witch doctor always a charlatan?

Understanding the healthy city

"To improve the health of the city environment and its inhabitants demands an understanding of the city as a whole, how it works, how the different parts fit into the whole, where the infrastructure and basic service systems work, and where they do not. Awareness of historical precedents helps such an understanding. Solutions require collaborative efforts between people and their governments (local, regional, national), politicians, community organisations, and professionals. Virtually all sectors of government and business have an effect on health. Government has a particular responsibility to establish the legal and institutional structure to encourage healthy and sustainable development, using various types of incentives and disincentives. Consideration of health requirements must be an integral part of urban development."

Quoted from the *Report of the Panel on Urbanisation*, by the WHO Commission on Health and Environment, published in 1992.

The Urban Economy

All cities, even the poorest, have vast human resources. A 'healthy city' is one which taps that energy and uses it for the benefit of the maximum number of people.

Free market energy

Urban managers have to strike a balance between regulation of business activity and market freedom. Those most concerned with social justice often distrust business enterprise, suspecting it of selfishness and greed. Yet the energy and know-how of entrepreneurs are vital to urban renewal. And taxation of business profits helps to fund municipal services.

Small businesses, working in both the formal and informal sectors, provide the lifeblood of cities. But they may present the governing authorities with even more serious obstacles to change than powerful multinationals. Monitoring a few large companies to ensure that they follow certain rules to protect public health and well-being is one thing. Applying such rules to myriads of small businesses is very much harder.

Richard Buckley

A city cannot be genuinely healthy for its inhabitants unless it has a vigorous economy, able to provide employment for all those who want to work. Having a large number of unemployed or underemployed people in a city is bound to be a recipe for trouble as well as ill-health. Of course, building a success-ful urban economy is easier said than done. Even the most general concepts, such as market forces, have to take into account local differences in resources, education and culture.

There are some 'businesses' which are part of the basic infrastructure of a city – energy supply, provision of water and sanitation, transport, the collection, treatment and disposal of waste, road construction and repair, telephone links, etc. Traditionally, these have been publicly owned. But more and more city authorities have privatised all or part of these activities, in the belief that they are more efficient than state monopolies.

Introducing an element of competition has indeed sharpened efficiency in many instances. Private/public partnerships have become all the rage in urban management – a move encouraged by most international agencies.

Until recently, it was thought that the best way to deal with industrial pollution of cities was to remove the industries to rural sites where they would cause less damage. But the consequence was to reduce both urban jobs and the incentive for industries to stop polluting. A more enlightened view is to clean up the industries so that they no longer pollute the environment. Thus they can operate in urban areas without causing damage to health.

It's not enough just to look at a city's commercial success. Money may be short but human resources tend to be vast. Using them effectively can transform a city. Many urban innovations are aimed at just this

---

Bombay – a great trading centre, with millions of poor slum dwellers

Bombay is India's leading financial centre and the largest port city in Asia. Industrialis-ation began with the opening of the first cotton mill in 1851. The population of Greater Bombay grew from about 1 million in 1911 to 3 million by 1950 and 10 million by 1995. The Bombay Metropolitan Region, embracing over 900 villages and 19 urban centres, now has some 15 million inhabitants. Population density on the central island city, which is built on largely reclaimed marshland, is the highest in the world. Luxury apartment towers stand alongside high-density squatter settlements and pavement dwellers. Over half the population live in slums.

One of the noisiest cities in the world, levels exceed 80 decibels at busy intersections (65 decibels being regarded as a tolerable limit). The bus system carries almost 5 million passengers a day, rail trips over 7 million a day. There is severe air pollution, with vehicle emissions contributing 60% of toxic fumes and industry 30%. Most sewage is discharged untreated into creeks or coastal waters. Water pollution has become a major health hazard. Land is scarce and prices high. Some 75% of the city's households have no legal tenure.

Despite all this, Bombay continues to grow, attracting yet more people to the chaotic bustle of its vast urban community. Like other efforts to get people to move out of established cities (such as Cairo and São Paulo), the attempt to develop a new 'twin city' across Bombay harbour has had limited success.

Public-private partnerships – and good leadership

The best-run cities are those where private and public sectors work in partnership rather than in conflict. A good mayor can make a big difference, especially if he or she has the backing of recent electoral success – and knows how to get different interest groups to work together.

These young porters, with the headstraps they use for carrying loads, are just two of the millions of children who work in the world's cities. They should be at school. But can their parents afford the investment which education requires? And what if their parents have abandoned them – an all-too-common fate for city children from Lima to Moscow.

target. Supposing for example that the city paid people to plant trees in their own neighbourhood? Wouldn't they be more likely to do the job properly and look after the trees well than if the local authorities did the job for them? Other ideas, from Bangkok's "Magic Eyes" anti-littering campaign to São Paulo's community wholesale markets, are also aimed at using grassroots energy to improve urban life.

Land ownership is a critical issue. Much urban development is informal and takes place on land to which the users have no title. City authorities have often been forced to give up the idea of preventing such 'development' and have taken instead to legalising tenure and providing services – another way of boosting the self-help engine which drives most human beings.

Some argue that economic success is a prerequisite of urban health. Only when a certain level of prosperity

has been achieved can the city begin to look at ways to improve its health. For example, the city of Kaohsiung in Taiwan, having achieved wealth through industrial growth – and having ruined its local environment – is now attempting to reinvent itself as a healthy city with its "Kaohsiung 21" project.

Others argue that long-term economic success actually depends on getting a proper balance between commercial, human and environmental factors. A city which ignores the social and environmental consequences of economic growth sows the seeds of its own destruction. Decaying inner cities are one symptom of this problem.

Part of the attraction of the 'healthy cities' concept is that it builds into urban development 'non-economic' benefits which are very important to human beings, such as health, social well-being, community pride and a pleasant environment.

Learning how to manage urban revival – an experiment in Cairo

Improving living standards in a slum area is not just a question of pouring in money. Experience has shown that urban development programmes are unlikely to succeed unless the people directly concerned are involved at every stage from planning to implementation. This example shows how one UN-sponsored urban development project in Cairo embodies the new 'grassroots' approach.

The Gamalia area of Cairo is a densely populated community of narrow, twisting streets and numerous small businesses, often involving family workshops employing children. The area, close to the famous bazaar district known as Khan el Khalili, includes a number of fine Muslim monuments which are in a poor state of repair. The project to reinvigorate the area began with a detailed study of over 100 extended families and some 160 workshops and small retail businesses. About 50 people from this community were invited to an all-day meeting to identify the main problems and opportunities facing the area. About a month later, 15 of the group, almost half of them women, were asked to attend a three-day session to pinpoint the most urgently needed changes. Three key priorities were agreed – (1) garbage collection; (2) a training centre for women to learn craftwork; and (3) tourism facilities which would enable local people to sell products and services to visitors.

At first, community representatives assumed that it was the government's responsibility to fulfil these three basic needs. But they soon realised that the only way to make it all happen was to do it themselves. With help from local UN representatives, they formed a new NGO – the Sustainable Development Association for Gamalia – which is now leading the community's efforts to regenerate the area. Preparation of a land use map revealed anomalies such as a coal-drying area, which would have been better sited in the desert, and a sacking repair building whose owner was willing to change use to a tourist centre. Another building was identified by Cairo's Antiquities Department as a site for the Gamalia Association headquarters, enabling it to be officially registered with the authorities. By providing a link between the energy, local knowledge and motivation of the community and the enabling powers of the municipal government, the Association should make it easier for self-help in Gamalia to succeed.

The Human City

There is no simple formula for urban health. Each city has its own blend of physical and social needs. Human well-being should be the common goal. But is it?

The physical environment, the social environment

People feel good when they are in pleasant physical surroundings. Gardens induce more well-being than car parks. So why do so many cities make more provision for motor vehicles than for people? Social integration – with family, friends, community – contributes strongly to the 'feelgood factor'. A divided society is an unhealthy society.

Open space, trees, grass, flowers, beautiful buildings, pedestrianised areas – such combinations increase a sense of human well-being in cities. By contrast, the urban jungle of concrete flyovers and residential towers increases alienation. In such depressing surroundings, it is hard to feel healthy or well-disposed to one's fellow beings. No wonder that violence and degradation so often accompany urban blight.

A healthy city would give the lie to Thoreau's observation that cities are places where millions of people are lonely together. No city can expect to make all its inhabitants happy, but some are much better than others at providing an environment which generates well-being. A neighbourhood without parks, or tree-lined squares, or cafes, or shops or leisure facilities cannot provide the kind of social interaction that can make city life so enjoyable – and healthy.

At the most obvious level, an unhealthy urban environment is one where disease is rampant. Cholera, typhoid, measles, diarrhoea, bronchitis – all are common in some cities, especially in Africa, Latin America and south Asia. In rich countries, many cities display other signs of ill-health – persistent street crime, litter, beggars, graffiti, drug addicts, scruffy children sleeping in doorways. Such symptoms reveal a malady far more difficult to cure than cholera or malnutrition.

Big cities have always been plagued with health problems affecting both mind and body. But there is much greater awareness now of the complexity of cities and the interlocking physical and social factors that affect health. For those urban managers who want to improve things, there is plenty of experience to draw upon.

Kuching (see box on page 15) is a small city which has had the good sense to look ahead and shape its own destiny. Indeed, the healthy cities programme is taken so seriously in Malaysia that it is co-ordinated from the office of the prime minister. Many thousands of cities throughout the world could benefit from the kind of communal involvement and progressive thinking shown by Kuching.

For the world's 50 or so mega-cities, it is probably too late for such grand visions. Governments can only tinker with the huge living machine that a city of 10-20 million people becomes. Yet, even in these mammoth conglomerations, planning is essential to provide an overall framework within which local communities can pursue their

Richard Buckley

Investing in health

An unhealthy population is a drag on the economy and on society in general. As the WHO argues, "health should be regarded as an investment and not as an expenditure". Aside from the moral issue, it is bad economics to allow a large section of a city's population, especially its young people, to live with ill-health or malnutrition. A robust economy depends on a healthy workforce.

various projects for improvement. The same basic principles apply – participation, openness, equity.

In Chittagong, Bangladesh, the Healthy Cities Programme, launched in 1993, has brought the poor into the urban renewal process in a way that never happened before. No-one ever thought to ask the people what *they* wanted. It was assumed that the authorities knew what was best for them. There is now a Slum Dwellers Forum, helping to represent the million or so people who live in the city's 110 slum areas.

The process of bringing together the various interest groups was "anything but a smooth process" according to the WHO's magazine *World Health*. Behind this oblique phrase lie all the tensions of getting

different interest groups to work in co-operation with each other.

For many cities, such multi-level participation is a worrying novelty. There may be great resistance to involving certain groups in the decision-making or planning process. Yet experience shows that a healthy city is one where all citizens feel that the city "belongs to them". Failure to meet the needs of all interest groups puts a city's health at risk.

What makes a city healthy?

According to the World Health Organisation, a healthy city:

* has a clean, safe physical environment

* provides safe and durable supplies of food, water and energy, and efficient waste disposal

* through a diversified, robust, innovative economy, meets the basic needs of all citizens for food, water, shelter, income, safety and work

* has a strong, mutually supportive, integrated, non-exploitative community, in which different organisations work in partnership to improve health

* involves the community in local government by enabling its citizens to work together to shape the policies that affect their lives generally and their health and well-being in particular

* provides entertainment and leisure activities that facilitate interaction and communication among its citizens

* values its past and respects the diverse cultural heritage and specificities of its citizens, regardless of race or religion

* provides easily accessible and good quality health services

* rests on a sustainable ecosystem.

Judged by these criteria, how many of the world's cities – either in the developed or developing world – are really "healthy"?

Kuching, Malaysia – an ambitious vision

" *A well-planned, vibrant, landscaped garden city, endowed with a rich artistic, scientific and educational culture. A bustling city with a flourishing and resilient industrial economy, yet clean, unpolluted. A safe city, offering a standard of living affordable by all its citizens. A city managed efficiently and enjoying state-of-the-art communication, information and mass transport technology and providing ready access to services, utilities and recreation areas. A city that is dynamic and attentive to its people's needs and constitutional rights.*"

Such was the grand plan envisaged by the people of Kuching for the future of their fast-growing city.

Kuching has grown from a small trading post to a city of some 250,000 people. In 1994, its two municipal councils for the north and south administrative areas decided to work with the Malaysian state health department and the WHO to identify what was needed to make Kuching a healthy city. In February 1995 a "healthy city week" was organised to canvass opinion and ideas from people at all levels of Kuching society. Pet hates included the public transport system, while Kuching's parks, shops and night markets were the most popular benefits offered by the city.

Feedback was reviewed at a "healthy cities conference" which gave the go-ahead to a five-year action plan covering almost every facet of city life – better public transport, temporary housing of construction workers, dealing with problems of vagrancy, squatting and crime, building of drains, roads and schools, artistic and cultural amenities, and so on. Work is now going ahead to implement the plan. Though it is too early to judge its results, the strong support of the central government for such initiatives, the fact that so much effort is devoted to community involvement – and to taking expert advice – bode well for the future of Kuching. It has already won credit for being the cleanest and most beautiful city in Malaysia.

Bibliography

Sources

Sources for this issue have included:

The Business of Sustainable Cities: Public-private partnerships for creative technical and institutional solutions (part of the proceedings of the Second Annual World Bank Conference on Environmentally Sustainable Development, co-sponsored by the World Bank and EarthKind and held at the IMF, Washington, September 1994); *Encyclopaedia Britannica;* Friends of the Earth; *Habitat Debate* (the journal of the UNCHS); *The Independent;* International City/County Management Association (ICMA); The International Healthy Cities Foundation; Mega-Cities Project; *Metropolitan Planning and Management in the Developing World: Spatial decentralisation policy in Bombay and Cairo*, United Nations Centre for Human Settlements, 1993; *Rapid Urban Environmental Assessment: Lessons for cities in the developing world*, by Josef Leitmann, Urban Management Programme, World Bank, 1994; *Report of the Panel on Urbanisation,* WHO Commission on Health and Environment, 1992; Together Foundation.

Books and other publications

The Challenge of Urbanisation: *The world's largest cities,* United Nations, 1995 (294 pages; ISBN 92-1-151301-4; $29.00)

These profiles of 100 of the world's large cities – from Abidjan (Côte d'Ivoire) to Yangon (Myanmar) – reveal tremendous diversity. There are numerous insights into the practical problems faced by major cities around the world and the steps taken to resolve them. Water and sanitation, transport and waste management are recurring themes. As the study points out, "A major solid waste problem in cities in developing countries is not one of disposal or recycling but rather of the failure to collect garbage in the first place. Unaccounted-for-garbage – i.e., the difference between the amount of waste generated and the amount collected – is usually over 30 per cent and may constitute 50 per cent of the total."

Other revealing statistics: half the houses in Addis Ababa (population 2.2 million) have earth or mud floors (and most have corrugated iron roofs); 20% of Amsterdam people rely on bicycles for transportation; 50% of growth in Athens since 1945 has been illegal development (with exposed tie rods on concrete rooftops showing the intention to add extra floors when needed);

28% of Karachi's buses are out of service at any given time (because of breakdowns, maintenance problems, etc.); only 20% of houses in Khartoum are connected to the sewerage system; 500,000 people in Kinshasa have no access to public transportation and must walk for miles to reach work or health facilities; some of Lima's schools, designed for 1,000 pupils, are forced to accommodate 10,000 on split shifts; air quality in Los Angeles is unhealthy on two out of three days; New York generates over 23,000 metric tons of waste *per day*; about 90% of the 1.6 million commuters who travel to central Tokyo every day get there by rail.

Smog Alert: *Managing urban air quality*, by Derek Elsom, Earthscan, 1996 (226 pages; ISBN 1-85383-192-1; £14.95)

This excellent study of urban air pollution points out that 1.6 billion people worldwide could be at risk from breathing city smog. This puts urban air pollution alongside acid rain, ozone depletion and global warming as a major environmental issue. The book looks at the scale and causes of urban smog and suggests ways of achieving and sustaining healthy urban air. The book is full of up-to-date facts and real life examples which show the difficulties faced by urban managers trying to reduce air pollution. For example, an Indonesian scheme to ban vehicles from the city centre unless they had two or more occupants "started a new business, with young boys hiring themselves as extra passengers on the edges of the cities". The *Hoy No Circula* scheme in Mexico City (see page 5) led many families to buy a second, usually older and more polluting, vehicle so that they could drive on the day forbidden to their main car.

Urban Health in Developing Countries: *Progress and prospects,* edited by T. Harpham & M. Tanner, Earthscan, 1995 (228 pages; ISBN 1-85383-281-2; £14.95)

A collection of academic-style essays, by a variety of health and urban management experts, which deal with the latest thinking on urban health in the developing world. The aim is to take an integrated interdisciplinary approach, bearing in mind the disappointing results of earlier development efforts, which tended to focus on specific technical projects. Brief case studies include experience from Santiago, Dar es Salaam, Kampala, Dhaka and Bombay. This is a book for academics, professionals working in the field and serious students only.

Environmental Innovation and Management in Curitiba, by Jonas Rabinovitch with Josef Leitmann, Urban Management Programme, UNDP, the UNCHS and the World Bank, 1993 (63 pages; No ISBN number)

Curitiba is often held up as an example of how a city can grow while retaining its humanity and environmental health. During the last 20 years, as this UN working paper notes, "green space per capita has increased one-hundredfold (from $0.5m^2$ to $50 \, m^2$ per citizen), an increase that is all the more amazing given that it took place during a period of rapid population growth". Other innovations are described, including the planning process, the transport system, the waste recycling programme and policies for sewage treatment, industrial pollution control and the preservation of green space and cultural heritage.

A key factor in Curitiba's civic development has been the role of its mayors, notably Jaime Lerner (now governor of Parana), who, for over 20 years, have persisted with a coherent plan for the city's development, stressing the importance of people and ecology. In a very real sense, Curitiba belongs to its people – who present a wide mixture of income levels and ethnic groups. Poverty is common but less oppressive than in many other cities. As the authors point out, "the difference between these (low-income) families and those living in other Brazilian state capitals is not the condition of poverty itself, but the level of services and the degree of participation in community activities offered to these families by the city".

World Development Report 1993: *Investing in health,* published for the World Bank by Oxford University Press, 1993 (332 pages; ISBN 0-19-520890-0; £14.99)

The World Bank's annual report has a different theme each year. The 1993 report focused on health and contains a wealth of information about the "interplay between human health, health policy and economic development".

Other relevant publications include:

The Life Cycle of Urban Innovations, Elwood M. Hopkins, Urban Management Programme, 1994; *Urban Management Programme Annual Report 1994; Urban Air Pollution in Megacities of the World,* UNEP/WHO, 1992; *The International Drinking Water Supply and Sanitation Decade: End of decade review,* WHO 1992; *Cities: Life in the world's 100 largest metropolitan areas,* Population Crisis Committee, 1990.

Understanding Global Issues

Recently published briefings:
Marine Pollution: The poisoning of the seas
Europe 1945-1995: Hopes and realities
The Motor Car: Preparing for the 21st century
The New Brazil: Breaking with the past?
The Troubled Balkans: History's dangerous
   legacy
The World of Islam: Tradition, change, conflict
Solar Energy: Harnessing the power of the sun

Coming next:
Russia and Its Neighbours: Uneasy
   relationships
Controlling Global Trade: The role of the
   WTO
The New Germany: Six years after
   reunification
The Rise of Poland: How much stability in
   central Europe?

Where to obtain *UGI*

UNITED KINGDOM and WORLDWIDE
except the countries listed

Understanding Global Issues Ltd
The Runnings, Cheltenham, GL51 9PQ
Telephone: +44 (0) 1242 245252
Fax: +44 (0) 1242 224137

CANADA
Weigl Educational Publishers Limited
1902 - 11 Street SE,
Calgary, Alberta T2G 3G2
Telephone: 1 (800) 668 0766
Fax: (403) 233 7769

UNITED STATES OF AMERICA
American Forum for Global Education
120 Wall Street, Suite 2600
New York, NY 10005
Telephone: (212) 742 8232
Fax: (212) 742 8752

AUSTRALIA
Mentone Educational Centre
24 Woorayl Street,
Carnegie 3163 Victoria
Telephone: (03) 9563 3488
Fax: (03) 9563 4567

Subscriptions

UGI is available either as a briefing alone, or as an "education pack": a copy of the briefing plus a very large wall poster (1188 x 840 mm) of the centre-spread topic chart, folded into a clear plastic A4 wallet.

UK prices, from 1st April 1996:	**Briefing**	**Pack**
Subscriptions (the next 10 issues)	£27.50	£69.50
(reduced rates available for multiple subscriptions to the same address)		

Single issues

Back issues (1992-3)	£1.75	£5.95
Back issues (1994-5)	£2.50	£6.95
(minimum order 5 assorted titles)		

Additional
notes

Over 40 briefings already published, 10 new ones every year ...

For a full list, and details of your local prices, subscription rates and <u>special offers</u>, just put your name and full address on a postcard or fax, mark it "UGI", and send it to the distributor for your country.

Notes on the topic map (centre pages)

Figure 1: Urbanisation by country and location of principal cities

The pace of urbanisation in recent decades has been remarkable. Most big cities are now in the developing world. The map shows how few countries still retain a predominantly rural population. They include Afghanistan, Bangladesh and Burkina Faso (80% rural), Papua New Guinea (82%), Uganda (87%) and Burundi and Rwanda (94%).

This list also includes some of the world's poorest countries, supporting the theory that urbanisation is good for economic development. Certainly, some of the world's richest countries are highly urbanised – for example, Singapore (100% urbanised), Germany and Australia (85%) – but the theory should not be pushed too far. A third of Switzerland's population lives in the country. France (73% urbanised) is a good deal richer than Spain (81%).

In broad terms, however, there is a striking parallel between comparative GDP per head and the level of urbanisation in different countries. Whether GDP is a proper measure of quality of life is another matter.

Figure 1 also shows the location of all urban agglomerations of over one million people, based on UN figures published in *World Urbanisation Prospects* in 1993. A total of 287 cities are shown for 1995, up from 80 in 1950.

The 20 biggest cities are shown separately, with growth between 1970 and 1990, and the estimated population for 2010.

The list of the world's 20 largest cities in 1950 is strikingly different:

New York	12.3
London	8.7
Tokyo	6.9
Paris	5.4
Moscow	5.4
Shanghai	5.3
Essen	5.3
Buenos Aires	5.0
Chicago	4.9
Calcutta	4.4
Osaka	4.1
Los Angeles	4.0
Beijing	3.9
Milan	3.6
Berlin	3.3
Mexico City	3.1
Philadelphia	2.9
St Petersburg	2.9
Bombay	2.9
Rio de Janeiro	2.9

Detailed information on comparative health standards in 1950 is unavailable. However, it can be assumed that the poor, especially in the non-industrial countries, lived grindingly wretched lives in 1950. Some health standards, such as infant mortality and life expectancy, have greatly improved since then. Other 'quality of life' standards, such as pollution, overcrowding and crime, have probably got much worse. Some diseases, notably smallpox, which has been totally eliminated, have less of an impact. Others, notably Aids, have emerged. National and WHO programmes have resulted in large health gains, yet poverty and burgeoning population have made the fight against disease a continuing challenge. Urbanisation makes mass health programmes, such as clean water supply, sanitation and immunisation, much cheaper per head of population affected. At the same time, the spread of disease is made more likely by the density of urban populations and unsanitary conditions.

Figure 2: Comparative quality of life in selected cities

In 1990, the Washington-based Population Crisis Committee (later renamed Population Action International) published *Cities*, a comparative study of living standards in the world's 100 largest metropolitan areas. Ten indicators were used:

* public safety (murder rate as a general guide to the level of physical violence);

* food costs (proportion of household income spent on food – a general guide to wealth and poverty);

* living space (number of people per room – a general guide to overcrowding);

* housing standards (availability of clean running water, sanitation, garbage collection services and electricity);

* communications (number of working telephones);

* public health (infant mortality rate – a general indicator of public health);

* peace and quiet (level of ambient noise);

* traffic flow (rush hour congestion);

* clean air (level of pollution by photochemical smog).

Figure 2 shows four of these indicators for ten important cities in different parts of the world. Note that air quality standards for Lagos and Dhaka are estimates.

The *Cities* survey was based on the situation in 1989. Despite the years which have since passed, Figure 2 probably still gives a fair picture of comparable living standards in the ten selected cities.

Urbanisation by region 1950 to 1995 (with forecast for 2025) in %

	1950	1965	1995	2025
Africa	14.5	20.6	34.7	54.1
Asia	16.4	22.2	34.0	54.4
Europe	56.2	63.8	75.0	84.5
North America	63.9	72.0	76.4	85.0
South America	43.2	55.9	78.0	87.5
Central America	39.7	50.2	68.3	80.1
Caribbean	35.3	43.3	61.7	74.3
Former USSR	41.5	52.8	68.1	80.4
Oceania	61.4	68.6	70.9	77.1
World	**29.3**	**35.5**	**45.2**	**61.2**

Source: *World Urbanisation Prospects*, United Nations, 1993

Additional notes

Habitat

The first Habitat conference was held in Vancouver in 1976 and led to the founding, in 1978, of the United Nations Centre for Human Settlements (UNCHS or Habitat), based in Nairobi. Habitat focuses on managing urbanisation in order to make the world's cities, towns and villages healthy, safe, equitable and sustainable.

The UNCHS, along with the UN Development Programme and the World Bank, runs the "Urban Management Programme" to improve urban efficiency and living standards, especially for vulnerable groups such as women and the poor. Habitat currently has over 220 on-going technical co-operation programmes in close to 100 countries. The technical co-operation activities of Habitat are the most highly leveraged of any UN agency. Over the last five years, Habitat projects have consistently resulted in national investment commitments ranging from $1 billion to $3 billion annually.

Yet these are puny amounts compared with the levels of investment required to solve global problems of urban deprivation. In 1990 it was estimated that 600 million people living in cities were being threatened by lack of food, clean water and shelter. The number is even larger now. Overcrowding, piles of garbage, polluted air, poor working conditions and street violence add to the stresses on the urban poor.

Healthy Cities Programme

Launched by its European office in 1986, the WHO's Healthy Cities Programme has spurred numerous initiatives around the world, providing a catalyst for many positive changes in urban management. The theme has been taken up by major cities, by urban neighbourhoods (such as the "Healthy Suburbs" of Montreal), and even by islands, villages and schools. By focusing on health – an objective which is non-controversial – communities are able to build the foundations of co-operation between different interest groups. This can then lead on to other improvements in urban life – all of which affect health (e.g., transport, housing, employment prospects).

By April 1996, over 1,000 cities worldwide had joined the Healthy Cities Programme

under WHO auspices. They include both large cities (such as Amman, Chittagong, Johannesburg, Liverpool, Montreal, St Petersburg and Tehran) and smaller cities such as Kuching in Malaysia, Togliatti in Russia, Kaohsiung in Taiwan and Rufisque in Senegal. In Curitiba, Brazil, the mayors of over 20 cities recently signed the "Carta de Curitiba", pledging to develop and support a Brazilian healthy cities network.

In short, the Healthy Cities Programme has caught the imagination of city managers across the world. Though it began in industrialised Europe, it has now spread to all parts of the world, appealing as much to developing countries as it does to the richer nations. Among the dozens of countries where the programme is gaining ground are Bangladesh, China, Egypt, Iran, Malaysia, Mexico, Nigeria, Pakistan, Peru, Tanzania, Thailand and Tunisia.

The Healthy Cities Programme is part of the wider strategic goal of the WHO, spelled out in 1977: "the main social target of governments and the WHO ... should be the attainment by all citizens of the world by the year 2000 of a level of health that will permit them to lead a socially and economically productive life". The goal of "health for all" may be optimistic – it clearly won't be achieved by the year 2000 – but the target is well worth pursuing.

International City/County Management Association (ICMA)

An international municipal management institute based in Tempe, near Phoenix, Arizona. Founded in 1914, ICMA is a professional and educational association for more than 8,000 appointed administrators and assistant administrators serving cities, counties, other local governments, and regional entities around the world.

International Union of Local Government Authorities (IULA)

Founded in 1913, the IULA is a worldwide organisation of local government representatives, which now has members in more than 80 countries. Like ICMA, its activities include the international exchange of information and ideas concerning best practices in city management.

Mega-Cities Project

The New York-based Mega-Cities Project was established in 1987 as a 'technology transfer' vehicle for innovative ideas. Mega-Cities has fieldsite teams set up in 20 cities worldwide (Bangkok, Beijing, Bombay, Buenos Aires, Cairo, Calcutta, Delhi, Jakarta, Karachi, Lagos, London, Los Angeles, Manila, Mexico City, Moscow, New York, Paris, Rio de Janeiro, São Paulo and Tokyo). These teams are constantly identifying innovative approaches to urban problems, so that they may be transferred and replicated. The goal is not only to find solutions to the problems faced by large cities, but to understand how new ideas are spread and the implications for deliberate social change.

World Business Council for Sustainable Development (WBCSD)

A Swiss-based NGO, representing over 130 companies from 36 countries inside and outside the OECD, the WBCSD works with the UN to provide "City Services", a packager of municipal projects for small businesses. Typical projects would involve the supply of services in water, waste management and energy. City Services carry out feasibility studies with municipal authorities and then present specific business opportunities to local entrepreneurs, freeing them from the need to carry out time-consuming and expensive investigations by themselves.

World Health Organisation (WHO)

The WHO was set up on 7 April 1948, a date marked each year by World Health Day. The WHO is one of the largest specialised agencies of the UN, with a budget of $1.9 billion a year. To fulfil its mandate – "Health for All" – WHO provides central clearing house and research services, carries out mass campaigns for the control of epidemic and endemic diseases, and promotes improvement of public health programmes of developing countries. Further information about the Healthy Cities Programme can be obtained from Greg Goldstein at WHO's headquarters:

20 Avenue Appia, CH-1211, Geneva 27, Switzerland.
Telephone: 41 22 791 3559
E-mail: goldsteing@who.ch

Healthy Cities: Improving urban life

Almost three billion people live in the world's towns and cities. Some of them enjoy a high standard of living, but most do not. The 1996 Habitat II conference, run by the United Nations Centre for Human Settlements, and the Healthy Cities Programme of the World Health Organisation are part of ongoing efforts to improve urban life around the world. What lessons have been learnt?

IN THIS ISSUE

£2.95 RRP

ISSN 1355-2988

ISBN 0-85048-964-4

9 780850 489644 >

Understanding Global Issues
Editor: Richard Buckley
Published by Understanding Global Issues Limited,
The Runnings, Cheltenham GL51 9PQ, England

Understanding Global Issues is based on a concept developed as *Aktuelle CORNELSEN Landkarte*, published by Cornelsen Verlag, Berlin. Sources for this issue are given on page 16. Other publication details are given on the fold-out flap.

Text and design copyright © 1996 Richard Buckley and
Understanding Global Issues Limited
Artwork: The Chapman Partnership
Cover picture: A view of Melbourne, Australian Tourist Commission
Consultants for this issue: The World Health Organisation

Printed on woodfree paper by St Ives (Plc)

Healthy Cities

Improving urban life

Understanding Global Issues

A periodic briefing with topic map, illustrations, charts, facts and analysis

Introduction

In 1900 only about 14% of the world's people lived in cities. Today the proportion is over 45% and rising. Global society is being transformed as millions of people move from the countryside to the cities. The urbanisation of mankind is perhaps the biggest social change in history. In the last five years the world's urban population grew by 320 million people – equivalent to 19 cities the size of New York. By 2025, the urban population is expected to reach 5 billion, of whom 77% will live in less developed countries.

Urbanisation is often seen in negative terms – overcrowded slums, traffic jams, dirty air, crime, etc. Much government effort has been devoted to turning back the tide of urban immigrants and persuading them of the joys of rural living. It has been a largely futile policy. Making a virtue of the inevitable would be a wiser course. The WHO's Healthy Cities Programme* recognises the huge importance of urbanisation, and its social and health consequences.

The World Bank is even fairly cheerful about the future of the world's cities, basing its optimism on the revolutionary changes taking place in technology (such as telecommunications and solar power); values (more concern for environmental issues and human rights); and participation (more grassroots involvement in urban projects).

For many of the people who live in urban conglomerations, such as Lagos, Bombay or Mexico City, the idea of a 'healthy city' must seem like a sick joke. Yet broadly speaking, people who live in cities are better off than their counterparts in the countryside. There would be no mass movement to the cities if people knew that life there was very much worse than in rural areas. This conclusion is borne out by the statistics. GDP per person and human development indices both tend to improve as a country becomes more urbanised.

Health is much more than just freedom from disease. "Health," as a Belfast city poster put it, "is a state of complete physical, mental and social well-being. It is feeling good about yourself – your surroundings – your city." In all too many cases, however, urban people do not feel good about themselves or their cities. In the rich world, the better-off city dwellers complain about traffic jams and crime, while low self-esteem is a common characteristic of those most inclined to urban violence. In poor countries, people lament the lack of water, sanitation, decent housing, fresh air, jobs.

'Top-down' solutions to these problems – projects agreed among bankers and experts and imposed upon communities – have often had disappointing results. Advisers have gradually turned to 'grassroots' methods, with more and more involvement of local communities. Such a shift is sometimes viewed with suspicion by governments, which see any attempt at decentralisation as a threat to their power.

Indeed, some believe that 'city states' could replace 'nation states' as the power centres of the future. In many countries a single large city dominates the economy. The city state of Singapore, voted the "world's best city for business" for ten successive years, shows how a poor urban area can become rich by careful planning and the unleashing of human resources. Regional metropolitan areas – Tokyo-Yokohama, Guangzhou-Hong Kong, New York-Philadelphia, Cairo-Alexandria – already wield enormous political and economic influence.

City managers are in touch with each other in a way that was never possible in the past. They share 'best practice' experiences at international conferences, via 'twin city' arrangements or through the Internet. There are global and regional networks for everything from urban crime prevention to waste water treatment. Some of these are inter-governmental but many others are private initiatives of NGOs and individuals.

The biggest 'facilitator' is the United Nations organisation. The UN, often impotent when it faces political violence, plays a genuinely valuable role in social and economic development around the world. Various agencies are involved in improving urban life, including the UN Development Programme, the World Bank, the World Health Organisation and the UN Centre for Human Settlements*, organiser of the Habitat II 'City Summit' in Istanbul in June 1996.

Development activity, which used to focus on technical solutions to specific problems – energy shortage, lack of clean water, susceptibility to disease, overpopulation – has evolved a more 'holistic' approach. This is a big step forward though it makes the challenge even greater, requiring consideration of such awkward issues as decentralisation.

Development has often been held back by the desire of central government to hold on to both power and purse strings. Getting central and municipal authorities to work together – while involving local communities, independent experts and international technology transfer groups – is a task which the UN is uniquely qualified to do.

* **See note on page 17**